Bachelard Interpreted 5

An Ocean of Purity

Frank Prem

Wild Arancini Press
2025

Publication Details

Title: An Ocean of Purity
ISBN: 978-1-923166-29-5 (p-bk)
ISBN: 978-1-925963-93-9 (e-bk)

Published by Wild Arancini Press
Copyright © 2025 Frank Prem
All rights reserved:

No part of this publication may be reproduced, stored in a retrieval system, or transmitted in any form or by any means, electronic, mechanical, photocopying, recording or otherwise, without prior written permission from the publisher and author.
A catalogue record for this book is available from the National Library of Australia.

Cover Concept: Wild Arancini Press
Cover Image AI assistant: Adobe Firefly

Let us all rise from the waters. Then sing.

CONTENTS

An Ocean of Purity

Introduction 1

Water and Dreams

rose 5
the brook 6
I, the water... 7
cultured 8
the sculpt... 10
with earth and water 12
a small cartography................................... 14
where are you going 15
as recorded.. 16
shallow waters 18
in repose.. 20
satisfying (the mirror)................................ 22
fragile touch 25
what an eye beholds................................. 26
peacock inquisition................................... 28
a wall of air.. 29
reflected and dreamed.............................. 32
nymph waters 34
breach 35
the scale-feather concept......................... 36
odd fish.. 38
a change in the water............................... 40
reflected magic... 42
shadow dancer.. 43

a swallow of shadows 44
the river 46
the flood 47
the serious work 48
let's call it sailing 50
distort 52
marine dream 54
the pool farewell 56
between two mothers 58
the circle 60
two trumpets 61
sea of change 64
sailing my boat (for the first time) 66
take a penny keep a penny 67
the writer commits a suicide 68
a futility of power 71
the downside of popularity (the drowning pool) 74
cover me in my element 76
immiscible you 78
a last greeting 79
alight below 80
above the water 81
night 82
an assurance 84
intonight 86
curved edges 87
alchemy: from a stone 88
a tock (with dali) 90
power over the rod 92
the pull of truth 94
dynamic hands #1 96

dynamic hands #2 98
what mother does 100
a decision about the seas 101
tide 102
over evolved 103
meditating (in heavy water) 106
the swimmer 108
it is 109
purified 110
the water 111
an ocean of purity : one drop of passion 113
pure water 115
difficult departure 116
word (1) holding 118
word (2) secret 120
nothing sweet 121
one last drop (to do some good) 122
will, of water 124
cleansed 125
losing sight of pure 127
stirring the soup 129
effects of the fountain 131
water 133
failure oceanic 135
only clean 137
from storyland 138
an uncoordination of gods 141
measuring 143
the resistance 144
rehearsing the wind 145
ambivalent water 147

    born of tides 148
    the ocean bled 150
    two challenges (1) the child at war 151
    two challenges (2) the turbulent green 152
    the champion 154

Bachelard Source Materials 157

Author Information 159

Other Published Works 161

What Readers Say 163

An Ocean of Purity

Introduction

French scientist and philosopher Gaston Bachelard (1884 - 1962) explored and examined poetics and poetry in great depth over the course of his lifetime, particularly examining the poetics of natural elements, of which he identified the four that are traditionally considered:

Fire

Water

Air, and

Earth.

In addition, however, he (effectively) identified two further elements, or dimensions, for his examinations:

Time, and

Space

The *Bachelard Interpreted* poetry series responds to each of these elements and dimensions, and also encompasses certain other writings undertaken by Bachelard, encompassing some of his further scientific and literary undertakings.

An *Ocean of Purity* takes Bachelard's explorations of the poetic possibilities inherent in the dreams and reveries inspired by water and liquidity.

The collection is an exploration of the fluid, changes of form and structure, meeting points between liquid and solid. It contemplates the nature of flow and of ebb, as well as the intersections between nature and nurture. It draws on the faith needed to entrust the future into the care of the present.

Note: *An Ocean of Purity* is one of a series of poetry collections inspired by the work of Gaston Bachelard. References to the Bachelard translations that have been relied on as source materials for this project are listed at the end of this book.

Water and Dreams

rose

in the garden
of darkness
a black flower
shines

find it
with your touch
and by smell

reveal it -
your knees
on the ground
hands
groping -
the old-fashioned way

feel yourself forward

can you see there
the black flower
of night

does she bloom yet
in the picture
that you hold
in your mind

sweet perfume
velvet dark

sensuous touch

the dark rose
upon you

the brook

come and laugh
with me
let's
you and I
run

we will froth
our dabbles

come and play
our path
wanders
and leads us both
to
merry times

I am bubbled
with excitement
you
are a splash away
from laughing
loud

listen
with my stones
and gravel
I make a song

come
sing here with me
let's you and I
together
run

and sing

I, the water

I am the water
of this stream

small river

I hold no colour
but my stone

my gravel

the creeping moss

gaze through me
to the sand
paddle me
in my shallows

follow
the sun-shaft
down
through the depth
of my excavations
until the light
turns
into patient waiting

I am the water
of your life

paddle through me
in your shallows

gaze
into the depths
that are your own

lose yourself in me

in you
I am the water

cultured

well
you see
this

this here . . .

he grasped the young shoot
firmly
in a gnarled left hand

this here
is nature

he used a quiet voice
calm
as though
speaking to cows
without wishing
to disturb them
just before the milking

his right hand
held a wickedly sharp
and relatively sterile
pruning knife

a deft movement
part wrist-twist
part slice
and he had removed
the bulk of the growth

another practiced movement
and he had established
receiving notches
in the root stock
that remained

    while this . . .

he displayed
a short stick
slender
but matching the thickness
of the root stock
notch
for notch

    . . . *this*

he said again
as he slathered the wounded wood
with his own patent
rooting slather
of both
nutrition and protection

    is culture

    and it will grow
    exactly
    the fruit
    that I want

he wrapped the treated wound
with a generous quantity
of grafting tape

    my *culture*

he laughed
and went on
to perform
the next graft
on the next tree

the sculpt

she spent days
she spent
weeks

kneading

moulding

massaging life
into the clay

not alive
no no
but
it grew
real

she put her hands —
hard
gentle —
to the shaping

in her mind
she saw nuance

with her hand
she made marks
indented and raised
impressions

potter's knife
and water bowl

common clay
uncommon vivre

a work of art

still crude
but
precise
for what she required

and now she knows

now she sees

there is no need
any longer
to *imagine*

the shape is there

and so . . .

she moves her mind
to bronze

with earth and water

in a way
it is a struggle

the task
of digging deep
inside himself
to bring forth the . . .

what

the essence
perhaps
of himself
to incorporate
into the work

to shape the clay
with a knowledge
that emerges from his fingers
and hands
rather than his mind

he weds himself
to the materials
the mixture of soil
and water
from which he seeks to extract
a kind of life

he is a sculptor
of stone
a modeller
of clays

he does not know
any other way
to perform his art
than this

he has seen the shape
of a naked man
in his stone

seen it clearly

today
he moulds the vision in clay
to ensure his forms
his proportions

the foreshortening

and before him emerges
in miniature
his statue

complete
though rough

he looks at it
as dispassionately as he is able

nods

yes
it is as he saw it

there is good
life
in this

he can rest
while the model awaits him

he cannot see

he has turned away

but a line
a shape
has moved

the small model
has acquired
a smile

a small cartography

the map of the world
can only be drawn
in dreams

a cartography
that sketches who
you are
where
you have been

where are you going

the paths
of the spirit
fade away
in daylight
can't be seen
at night

but
there they are
in your dreams

take your pen
take your paper

better draw them now
before
you wake

as recorded

as soon as she woke
she took her pen
and began writing

still in her mind
the dream
that she dreamed
was real

she remembered
the conversation that she'd had
the insights reached
word
for
word

and the knowledge
that the revelations
of that dream
would change her life
for good

she penned
until her account
was on the paper

satisfied
she lay down
to let exhaustion come

and from the land
of sleep
looked forward
to describing
what she had done

but she searched
in vain
through the worlds
of somnambulance

until she woke —
disturbed
and unrested —
and wondering why

she looked at the page
where she had written
so intently

and saw
just one line
alone
penned by her hand

    that dream
    is gone

shallow waters

the waters show
a beautiful man

he throws his mane
about his shoulders

watches closely
for the visual effect
of the flowing
of his hair

the waters show
the face
of a man
looking down
and smiling

he touches his face
pats the silvered hair
at his temples

above his brow

the waters
smile back at him
in assurance

encouragement

the waters show
a man
gazing down

reflect a sigh
of satisfaction

though time has passed
the waters continue
their reflection

An Ocean Of Purity

though time has passed
the waters
remain shallow

in repose

the mirror
in repose
faced a room
filled
with slumber

nothing came
and passed
without notice

dust
danced
devils motivated by the sun

nothin . . .

> *what is this*
> *who is this*

a woman

stood before it

neither slender
nor stout
nor so very tall

> *who is this*
> *is it*
> *me*
>
> *I move*
> *when she moves*
>
> *we are one*
>
> *I feel*
> *a rightness*
> *now she is*
> *before me*

An Ocean Of Purity

I am splendid
dressed
as I am
in these fine clothes

I can dance
I can whirl
look look
I can admire myself
when I glance back
across my shoulder

look at me
just look at me
I am so beauti . . .

the room
in repose
filled
with slumber

against a wall
facing the room
the glass of a mirror
showed nothing
passing by
without notice

satisfying (the mirror)

>   *I like myself well*
>   *I like me true*
>   *but*
>   *I would like me*
>   *better . . .*

the image
in the mirror
was too pink

too many
wrinkles

- white foundation
- dab rouge

>   *I like myself well*
>   *I like me true*
>   *but*
>   *I would like me*
>   *better . . .*

the image
in the mirror
wore thickened eyebrows

too
proletarian

-     pointy tweezers
-     serious thinning

>   *I like myself well*
>   *I like me true*
>   *but*
>   *I would like me*
>   *better . . .*

the image
in the mirror
wore drab eyes

too muddy

-       blue bright lenses
-       kohl mascara

I like myself well
I like me true
but
I would like me
better . . .

the image
in the mirror
had large ears

too low lobes

-       big round jewels
-       pierced earrings

I like myself well
I like me true
but
I would like me
better . . .

the image
in the mirror
had flat short hair

a little bit marsupial

-       pink bob wig
-       extensions

I like myself well
I like me true
but
I would like me
better . . .

the image
in the mirror
was a stranger

completely unknown

-     yeah nice
-     let's go

fragile touch

fragile fragile
his face
in the water

such wonder
dressed
in the familiar guise
of eyes
nose and mouth

brow and chin

he raises a hand
to touch his cheek

holds his breath

as the stream
caresses
his face

what an eye beholds

the eye
of the lake
looks up to the sky
from its place
high
in the mountains

sees clouds
and blue

birds flying
beneath the sun

in the distance
a storm
maybe

thinks:

> *the sky is big*
>
> *and*
> *so far away*
>
> *it is an immensity*
> *that never ends*
>
> *it is*
> *beautiful*

the sky
looks down from its height
sees the lake

clouds
and blue

birds flying

the sun

in the distance
there may be a storm
tonight

thinks:

> *that lake*
> *is so small*
> *but a lot*
> *like me*
>
> *I think*
> *it is beautiful*

peacock inquisition

the peacock stares
one hundred eyes

an inquisition
trembling
its intensity

but all it sees
is blue
blue blue

too aloof
to notice
me

a wall of air

they watched her
for a day
building
a cinderblock wall
made out of air
and out of water

from a bucket
and with a trowel
she laid
a foundation
and wet it

from a neat stack
beside her
a brick
of nothing
that she laid precisely . . .

so

the trowel
a thick mortar layer
of water
from the bucket

a brick of air
just . . .

so

her string-line
rose
row on row
as she labored

higher
and higher

missus
hey missus

what are you doing

asked one
perplexed

missus
what are you
building

asked another
more imaginative

taking a moment —
to wipe her brow
for the labour
was strenuous —
she replied

this
my little friends
as you can see
is a wall

when it is done
it will help me
keep a good separation
of what is
here
from what is
over there

I am sorry
little friends
to place a barrier
in your paths
but I do
what must be done

and so

she turned back
to her work
water-mortared another row

placed another brick
of wall-air
in its place

one small child
unnoticed
approached the wall

reached with a hand
to
touch it

to see what would happen

at the last
he could not do it

pulled his hand away
and retreated
to the safety
of his fellows
and burst into tears

reflected and dreamed

the dream he dreamed
was of himself

dreaming a life
his life
even as he lived it

lived it to the full

that
is what he dreamed
and it was so

in the mirror
what he saw
was
another mirror
reflecting
all
by the light of shining stars

so many
the mirror could not hold them

and bursting
they emerged
an overflow
over
the dreamer

who stood steady
and as still
as his dream was able

he took them
one and all
into himself

he took them
into a welling
of himself

in the mirror
he saw
another mirror
reflecting back a void
pure
a void
dark

he turned
once more
to face his dream
shining brilliant eyes
toward it

step
step
awake from sleeping

step step
the dream
is gone

nymph waters

as she watched
from the bank
a fish flew past

rainbow trout
by its markings

a bird swam by

it was heading
somewhere
wings wide
to ride in the current

in the reeds
unseen
a frog
ba-bonked the beat
and was answered
with a clear call

>   *I am coming*

but although
she heard
a nearby splash
she didn't see
a thing
for she woke
just then

stiff and cold
and uncovered

breach

he dared not
to look into the water

it is deep
and in the depth of it
no guarantees

things submerged
should stay
submerged

he would take
no chance
would not provoke
a deep thing
into breaching

the scale-feather concept

along the line
descending vertical
every fish
must swim

it is an idea
a requirement
that is immutable

along the line
horizontal
intersecting
every bird
must fly

it is an idea
a requirement
evident
without speaking it

at the collision point
oh woe
oh me
what a mess
of scales
and feathers

but the need exists
and the law
exists
and the fish
must fly
the bird
must swim
it's a concept
you see
some kind
of big idea

and away they go
almost
as they should
but with roles reversed
they are only
somewhat
scaled
and a little
feathered

odd fish

through the watery moods
of black night
odd fish
swim

unseen
but felt
like
a ripple

an eddy

dancing
across the skin

    (turn quickly)

        just there

    (turn quickly)

        over there

the fish of the night
swim swift

just   there

just there

the tide
of the night
ebbs assurance
away

the jetsam
is littered
on the nerves

An Ocean Of Purity

on a jangling headland
of fear
at the heart

and the fish swim by
unseen at all
whether tide has come in
or whether no

    hist

did you feel
that

did you feel that
did you see

a movement
         (turn quickly)

            just there

                just there

the odd fish
of night
swims

right
here

a change in the water

the water
that once ran
skipping
over stones
slipping through the moss

around fallen branches

ran
as though only a laugh
could slow it down

only a laugh
could catch it
make it chuckle

all the time
calling joy
up to the air

that water
that ran once
is a memory
brooking the hills

the water *now*
sits still
squat
and squalid

heavy
it might be deep

who can tell

a circle
of yellow suds
shows movement

rotation

An Ocean Of Purity

around it goes
and around

the water now
is ponderous

the water now
is laden

the water
now
is transformed
from bubbling
down
to slow blisters

and the weight of the world
is coloured green
and brown

the weight
of the world
is darkened
with lost delight

the bog tedium
of lost momentum

failed hope

reflected magic

will the lake
beseech the wind

the ripples
to recede

the sky
to present a settled face
of blue

the pine trees
to lean forward
around the water's edge

the cliffs
on the yonder side
in their best
variegated ochre
tints
to tall themselves
into elegance

all
to be still
and at best

for the magic
of a reflection
will now
be forged

shadow dancer

the shadow
in its glee
is a darkling dancer

stealthily
skip and blending
onto shapes across the wall
upon the road
each *where*
that it passes

leaning away

leaning always
away from the light

staying concealed
yet dancing

the shadow
dark-kiss
casanova

embraces
overcomes
im-penetrates

then moves along
its dark by-ways
to whelm
all over another patch
of the wall
of the road
of the alley

and overcome

im-penetrate

then creep
on

a swallow of shadows

every morning
the tree at the edge
of the stream

from first light
to dark

grows its shadows

like children
hidden inside the bark

beneath the leaves

as each day meanders
until the sun falls
from its circumnavigation
of the sky

one
by one
the shadows lengthen

one
by one
they
elongate

from trunk
to ground

from each individual leaf
down and then
to the water

the stream
ripples past delightedly
in its bed
unperturbed

every moment
is new water
flowing past

and as each darkness
touches
the water
ever-thirsty
drinks

takes it in
and takes it down
away
until
in the morning
the swallowing
concludes

and the tree
in the early
new sun

so much lighter

begins
the shadow work
again

while the stream
cannot stop
its gentle laughter
and new water
always
the new water
rolls clean
away

the river

she wept young hours
with every tear
she let fall
into the slow sweep
of the river
of regrets

drop by drop
time must fall
and melancholy
holds its own duration

hour by hour
the river flows
steadfast

days and days
into more days

she wept a year
in an outburst
of sobbing
wild

the river swelled
with each tear
that splashed

until
the water rose
high enough
to wet her feet

she was an old woman

her last days
still damp
on her cheek

the flood

he said

> every day
> the sorrow falls
>
> I am killed
> in the flood
> of shadows
>
> I do not
> come to life again
> in the morning
> with the sun
> but am the corpse
> on which
> the sorrow falls
> once more
>
> and I die
> another dying
> without ever finding life
>
> I die
> again
> in the flood

the serious work

she took her work
very seriously

she knew
the dependence that attached
to each verse

so
she poured a cup
placed paper
and her pen
then sat down
at the desk beneath the window
where the warm of the sun
might find her

and she wrote
the scene she saw
on the other side
of the glass

she wrote
the light
of the day

she wrote the love affair
of her neighbour
with her garden

of the few folk
attending chapel
these days

of their prayers

her pen
drew the picture
in words
of everything she could imagine
around her

on the paper
she rewrote
her little world
for the entirety
of a day

when she'd finished —
job done —
she leaned back
in the chair
and stretched

so tired

the work of
*the poe*t
she took
quite seriously

for if she failed
just once
to imagine the unfolding
of a day . . .

what might the world
come to be

what
would *her* world
be

let's call it sailing

let's call that
an Ocean

call this
a Boat

and
Sail . . .

you rise up
to catch Wind

we'll name the iron
Anchor

set it there
in kitty-corner
of the Bow

the bubbles
behind Stern
let's name
our Wake

and put the Blue
into the Ocean
before the Prow
of our little sailing Boat

rise
rise up
catch the Breeze

stow the Anchor
kitty-snug
against the Bow

behind
Bubbles rise
along our Wake

behind
the Bubbles rise
to be our Wake

distort

dark
and heavy
water

I pick you up
a stilled pool
in my hands

unmoving
except my reflection
grizzled as it is
shifting around to peer down
unbelieving

deep water
heavy laden
with filtered truths

every knowledge
a little chill
a thicker viscosity
until

saturation
comes in the end
and then
no more
and nothing new

only a still pool
reflecting me
clear
but shallow

if only I knew
what you know

what lies beneath

but all I see
from shifting around
is a reflected face
that no longer looks like

I am not
that man

I
cannot recognize him

who knew
the truth could be
so
so much
a distortion

marine dream

the creature thrashed

a seal

or a dolphin

thrashed again

raised a spray
that stopped him in his tracks
forced
to close his eyes

opened to a new scene

a line of guardian penguins
waddle-ambling formally
around the guard-line
of a dream

he closed his eyes

do not fear

a voice

a thrum

a resonation

you are the whale

I am
inside you

>   *you swallow me*
>   *and swallow me*
>   *yet*
>
>   *here*
>   *I am*

An Ocean Of Purity

thrashing before you
a creature
foolish without
my element

and you
my old
harpoon

will you dive now

thrust yourself
down
into the waters

dodging
the march
of swimming penguins
waiting the tables
on the perimeter

choose
from their menu

this is your dream

I
am inside you

the pool farewell

the departure
of the dead

in the wood
on a river

a little boat
alone
life's last adieu

taken in
at a calm place

taken slowly
riding low
to the last great maelstrom
the fall
that beats the boulders
in the receiving pool
below

farewell

over the falls
that beat
the last

farewell

spirit rise

boat
descend

the body
is a part of that

the shape
that is the spirit
the shape
within the hollowed tree

and the maelstrom left behind

adieu adieu
adieu

the farewell shape
that is the dead
in
what once
was a tree

what once
was alive

once was growing

the wood
is in the river

the wood
is a little boat
to bid this life
adieu

between two mothers

mother tree
encased her seed
in a pod she'd made
strong
to weather travel

mother tree
released the pod
with a seed inside
allowed it to fall
a small splash
into the water
she overhangs

oh stream

she cried

> *oh*
> *river*
>
> *you are a mother*
> *who flows*
> *but still*
> *a mother*
> *as I am*
>
> *oh stream*
> *oh stream*
> *receive*
> *this part of me*
> *into your keeping*
>
> *take it with you*
> *as you go*
>
> *leave it*
> *resting*
> *in the silt of some shallow*

on the bend
on one of your turnings

oh river
flow

mother
take my seed with you

away

the water
does not speak

flow only sings
in a murmur of water-song

but the pod
rides high
carried once around
as though
in an eddy

then bobbing
in soft corrugations
mid-stream
rides
in the direction
of the sea

a journey
begun with a prayer
and a beseeching

a wish
released into the faith
of a safe landing
downstream

the circle

a river

tributaries

a delta
flowing both ways

ebb and rise
and
ebb-rise again

draw that water
first
right down
to the end
then
draw that water
home

draw the water
send it round

around

around
the river flows

river
is a circle

life

around it flows

ebb-rise
and ebb-rise
river
flows around
again

two trumpets

at the falling
of the day
I sound the trumpet
slow

        pa   pa

at the recollection
of all that I've done

of the patient journey
through memory

        pa   pa

long ago
once upon a time
when I was young

        pa   pa

but now
with good-bye
in my sights

good-bye and bye
again

        pa   pa

the falling
of the day

        pa   pa

~

*at the rising
of the sun
I sound the trumpet
fast*

        pa   *pa*   *pa*

*there is so much
to be done*

        pa   *pa*   *pa*

*all
in just one day*

*and the sun
already
on the horizon*

        pa   *pa*   *pa*
        pa   *pa*   *pa*

I feel so alive

so energized

*everything
all so possible
and I
free to be doing it all*

        pa   *pa*   *pa*

*away
I have no moment
to linger*

        pa   *pa*   *pa*

I hear the trumpet call

*so good-bye
good-bye-and-good-bye now*

An Ocean Of Purity

        pa   *pa*   *pa*

it is the dawning
of day

        pa   *pa*   *pa*

sea of change

    captain

she said

    I have come in black
    I will say goodbye
    here
    at the foot
    of your gangplank

    when you leave
    I will be in mourning

    for the sea
    is the sea
    and the horizon
    the end of knowing

    of the world

she said

    captain
    I will not see you again

    for if you return
    even if
    you return

    I will still be
    as I am

    you
    a different man
    transformed by the salt
    of strange oceans

An Ocean Of Purity

when you go
the man you are
will go with you

I will mourn

she said

I will mourn

sailing my boat (for the first time)

who is the sailor
to sail my ship
beyond dreaming

who will be captain
if I
am the passenger now

flap the sails
while you tight up
the stay lines

point the prow
point the ship
to the blue

this is the last
this is the first
this is the journey
beyond mere dreaming

steer me straight
you solemn-faced boatman

steer to the sunset
steer straight
steer true

no *ship ahoy!*
there's just you and me
on the chart

solemn yes
but laughter too

behind is the old
ahead
is where we go

ahead
is the place I go

take a penny keep a penny

a penny
in your pocket

a penny
in your dreams

you don't know
when you will need it

you don't know
when
the waters may rise
to lap your feet

mother always said

> *clean clothing*
>
> *if something should happen*
> *you must be clean*

mother always said

> *take a penny*
> *my son*
>
> *keep a penny*
> *where you can find it*
>
> *if something*
> *should happen*
> *oh*
> *my dearest boy . . .*
>
> *take my penny*
> *in case*
> *the ferry comes*

the writer commits a suicide

he imagines the death

looks through the curtain
the veil
to the possible past

for

>motive

>slowly
>a picture emerges

>the small triumph
>the large failure

>moments of nothing
>but angst

>a progression
>plotted
>with a blue marker
>on squares
>running across
>then down
>on a rotatable whiteboard

>the storyboard

>ticking off justifications
>and steps
>towards intolerable
>feelings

>distress
>and dismay

>marked
>onto the board

An Ocean Of Purity

*and the idea
develops*

*gaining momentum
like a ball of snow
rolling
growing
at the head
of an avalanche*

rolling fast

rolling faster

unstoppable

*even if
he had wanted
to stop it*

*then
a search
a thorough search
for the most appropriate means*

a tool

*by pill
by rope
by the gun*

*maybe
in water*

*what method
most
suits the character*

*until
there . . .*

*the note has been typed
and the printer-paper
of a life
has breathed its last*

the novel sent off
with its sad but justified corpse
to be printed

he stares out
through the curtains
the veil
to a possible future

wonders
if it is worth
all the bother
in the end

a futility of power

into the water

bubbles rise
as a crowd
forming into a bubble-balloon

pop-pop-pop

a kind of anguish
released into the air

the steam

hiss-s-s

an angry threat
uttered into the midst
of a forced taming

close inspection
in mid-air

a to-and-fro
of turning
to better see

assess

then
the forge
again

the anger grows
the anger glows

the resistance
hugs itself
into a yellow-orange-red
possessive glower

that eye-lessly
identifies
a fee

in degrees of burn
and temperature

the anvil

    clang

the hammer blow

sparks
rising

    clang

the hammer blow

sparks flying

    s-s-s-s

the sizzle of a moment
is a moist bead
of fallen sweat

    clang

the sullen sound
torn
blow by blow
away from the nurturing
of power
brooking no song
but the blunt
of an echo

into the water

    hiss-s-s-s

bubbles
are released
into the air

the downside of popularity (the drowning pool)

they call it
the drowning pool

and this night
she goes there for the first time
to contemplate
as she submerges

it has been a popular place
for an end
to young girls

the still
beckoning water
white flowers

seclusion

so many
have made the descent
on the dirt path
that raises a fragrance
of forest
with each slippered step

she pushes her way
into the water
through the ill consideration
of early arrivals

only the determined
find a place

she pushes her way
into the water

through the diaphanous spread
of silky veils
and shifts and dresses
of early arrivals

An Ocean Of Purity

she pushes her way
to make a space
where she can wade
unimpeded
into the heart
of the pool

she pushes her way
with her feet
beneath the water
to clear
a little room
for her to settle

finally
personal space

surrounded
by a wall
a lacy-cloth logjam
of new arrivals
but
at least a space
that is hers alone
right now
before the wave
of new arrivals

a space
for her to contemplate
futility
and despair
as she submerges
to join with the throng
of early arrivals

cover me in my element

cover me
in air

I am surrounded

air
on my skin
on my eyes
in my lungs

inside of me

air
outside me
when it's done

~

cover me
with water

I am floating

water underneath
above
all about

water inside
will never leave me

water inside me
I am drowned

~

cover me
with earth

I am interred
below ground

soil
my mouth
my ears
soil
my fingers

buried
as one with earth
entombed

~

cover me
with flame

I am on fire

inferno
my beating heart

lick me kiss me
burn
I am a meld
within the haze

cover me in flame
till I am vapour

immiscible you

oil
is immiscible
with water

a rainbow
on the road
is proof

that opposites
may still be
attracted

attractive

not miscible
and
not the same
but
you
look so very good
with me

a last greeting

my brother
is a swan
he is a dolphin

he breathes
beneath the waters

he wakes
in the weak light
that is dappled dawn
below the waves

and calls the dead
of oceans
to him
calls the dead
to another fleeting moment

and he strengthens

the light brightens

the dead swim
breathe again
the fleet breath
of one moment

the waters clear
my brother
is the swan
he is the dolphin

he is life
among the waters

the dead greet him
when he calls
and then they go

alight below

I light my fire
in water

my flames make
their own space

I send my heat
rising
to the waves

my smoke
is plumed
my plume
is bubbles
my bubbles
are a bursting
of heat

I light my fire
in the water

I watch it burn

the smoke that rises
from the sea
is the flame I lit
below

the mystery
of a cauldron
deep down
in the middle
of an ocean

above the water

in the still
of the night
the phantoms wreathe
above the water

ravelling
unravelling
adrift

they retire
reluctantly
as day creeps
growing
lume by lume
until they are hidden

and the brightness
rules
for a short while

the brightness rules
only
for a short while

night will fall again
for the phantoms
to recall their misty shapes

they feed on the cold
on the night
on the heart

unravelling tendrils
they touch
they take

denser in the night
beware
the phantoms wreathe
in the dark of your dreams
above the water

night

she walks
after the light
has faded
in a long dress
blue-black
in satin

decorated
with the stars

she wanders
in no direction . . .

in all directions
here and there

everywhere

flowing over
all around
and moving on

all the time
she is moving on

sometimes
a golden moon
will lighten the way
casting over all
a glimmer
of warm

sometimes
there is nothing
to disturb the blue
in the black

only —
perhaps —
the stars as she walks

from behind her veil
she watches me

within her cloak
she may hide me
if I need that

when I need that

and I feel her then
in a shiver of spine
and know
she is come

she watches me

an assurance

the daytime
was his certainty

he sat high

> *overlooked*
> *supervised*

there were decisions
to make
and he
the small god
of the domain
to make them

inferiors —
cowed as they were —
acceded
agreed
nodded fervently

upheld
and supported

there was no doubt
there could be
no doubt

but night

the dread night

night was filled
with no-certainty
with the questions
that had no answers

An Ocean Of Purity

a lone electric globe
burned
through the dark hours
but provided only
a reservoir

a small reservoir
of *not-night*
around which the phantoms
and spirits
and gnawing doubts
of his own conjuring
fluttered
hovered
and peered
in an examination
he could not hope
to pass

the bottle
at his bedside
was certainly
only
one fifth
full

intonight

and where she walked
the daylight
followed after

into the night
each step

into the woman
each step

what was darkness . . .

taken
leaving light
behind

where she walked
the nighttime
became
her

she took it all
she breathed it all
until all of it
was
her

behind her
the day

bright

behind her
the sun

she walked into
the nighttime

behind her
was the sun

curved edges

there are no edges
in a curve

no angled corners

place a fingertip
anywhere
and begin

trace
around a finger

trace
across the hand

the length
of an arm

trace
with a finger
the body

there are no edges
on your curve

always
the end
is at
the beginning

alchemy: from a stone

his hammer *smacked*
a brittle
ineffective sound
against the granite

a little powder
a little flake

sometimes
he struck
a chisel into the stone
to achieve the same

he smacked
and he chiselled
until the powder
made a mound
at the bottom
of his crucible

with tongs
he placed the cup
upon the fire

there was nothing
he could see

just the shimmering
of heat waves

though he stared
until his eyes
began to weep

he was sure
so very sure
that if he watched
extra carefully
and noted
precisely . . .there would be
a trace

An Ocean Of Purity

a small trace
of mist
visible above the cup

and the water
that he knew with certainty
had to be there
would be
at last
released

a tock (with dali)

time
that melts
like french soft cheese

moulding seconds
minutes
hours

every *tock*
and every *tick*
to slide
seamlessly
into the wall

time
stuck like an adhesive
to hold up
the passing moments

time
that cannot maintain
its shape
instead
showing the signs
of a fade
into age

time
I recall you well

you are not the same
somehow
you seem a little
faster

I am slow

An Ocean Of Purity

time
my old pocket-watch
had a button
that I could twirl
that I could
turn
to restart

gone

time
alas the sun of days
has melted you
to blend
one fragment
into the next

and I recall
again
but still
I do not know
your name

power over the rod

at the forge
it is the turn
of heat

as hot as she can bear
but bear
she will

this is her place
and she wishes it
to scorch and to scald
and run
sweat
like a river

from the height
of her scalp
down the length of her torso

down her arms
to drip
and to sizzle
on the forge room floor

it is she
who stokes and builds
the red glare
beyond all capacity
all tolerance

then and there
right at the peak of all
the metal rod
a-glow
almost bending
of its own accord
of its own pliancy
almost
like red-gold butter

she exalts
when she raises it up
from the coals
to curl the air
and flavour the smoke
that she breathes

before she shapes
with a mighty pounding
of the hammer
down

the pull of truth

an example
of the truth
iss running
in a rivulet
down the pane of glass
in front of my eyes

breaking up
into a dotted trail
almost straight
but dodging
here and there
around imperfections

yet
remaining a faithful acolyte
of gravity

here comes
another one

same line
same dodge

this time
it is something like
two trains
that run on a single track

pause and run
pause and run

get your ticket punched
to ride
or
you can fly
like

another one
falls in a line
from cloud
to ground

a very fast drop
on a very fast line
that is different
yet
believes

has faith
in the same pull

that is gravity

and that
is a singular example
of truth

dynamic hands #1

the carpenter has
a geometric hand

he sets straight lines
he sets corners

hammers a nail
to keep the joint
both square
and strong

geometry
and construction

I
have no *square*
within me

I am soft lines
without angle

my hands caress
and coax
and shape

they sweep in curves
and arcs

they kiss
in curlicues
glide
through mud slurry

pressing firm

pressing light

texture
on texture

what's made is made
there is no sharp
there is
no edge

what's made
is made
by touch

made
is made
by
me

dynamic hands #2

I close my eyes
leave my hands
to work the clay

my fingers see
by touch

by press

round
around
I spin the wheel

dynamic hands

slippery
they slide
as though
of
the form

my thumbs
know
when to gentle in
my fingers
go on
caressing
and the clay
the sweet clay
yields
to the guiding touch

a tactile
sensual
absorption

behind closed eyes
I see the shape
dynamic hands are making

tenderness

creative love

mud
rising to become
bowl

fingers
coaxing
thin thin walls

the wheel
that is this dream
still turning

what mother does

mother soil
mother grass
mother tree

you nurture me

mother seed
mother flower
mother fruit

you nurture me

mother sky
blue

mother sky
grey

mother sky
thunder

mother lightning
and mother rain

my mother's storm
you nurture me

yes
nurture me

a decision about the seas

with the help
of the ocean
I will raise
the seas

into vapour
then
to cloud

just water
swirling in a turmoil
that I will make
filled with rage
until boiling

boil and burst
lightning strikes
uncontainable
a tempest

the wind blow
the wind cry

scream
moan
cry a mournful song

for when I have done
so much
all gone

cry while you scream
cry
while you sob

with the help
of the ocean deep
I will raise
the seas

tide

her feet
in the water

the waves
lapping
back and forward

low now
with the tide

sand
retreating
beneath her toes
pulling out to sea
as though it wants her

out there

the swell
is a rise and fall

here comes the high tide
the neap tide
a king tide
the mother of tides
to rock the water

back and forward

her feet
are in the water

the waves are lapping

the sand
wants to sweep her
away

away
on a receding tide

over evolved

a heavy man

no joke
this
he is
a heavy man

his suits are set
to *rumple*

sweat seeps
out from the pits of his arms
marching stealthy

he walks
a wide stance walk

ponderous
as a slow thought
in the middle of
the longest day

he does not fit
into the shape
of this world

he is
a struggle of awkwardness
this man

in the evenings
of summer days
he takes himself
to the public baths

battles free of his clothes
in the change room

a big towel

he carries
a big towel
draped across his shoulders
and down
to cover him enough
to reach poolside

sits
his feet
are in the water

he
is in the water
no sound
no splash

suddenly he
and the water
as one

he seals below
the surface

porpoises
for air

rays along
on the bottom
for a while

he feels light

he can turn
so quickly
move below
so easily

in the evenings
of summer days
he comes alive
in the water
laughs a trail of bubbles

watches them rise

he otters
on his back
a while

one day

one day
he is going to leave
the city

one day
he will go
to the ocean

abandon his big towel

gritted
in sand
on the beach

and he will
drift out
with the tide

in the evenings of summer days
he remembers

he remembers what it is
to be alive

meditating (in heavy water)

there is no rocking
in heavy water
no comfort to find
there

only
floating

the silence
is loud

a resounding nothing
that fills
the chamber

rebounding nothing at all
where it seems
thoughts should be

    [splash]

a hand down
the sound dies away
leaves an empty space behind

a **[splash]** shape
in the darkness

meditate
on going mad

meditate
on empty

heavy water
keeps you afloat
heavy water drags down
everything

meditate
on going mad

there's no rocking
in heavy water

the swimmer

she swam between the clouds
in an ocean
of air
in the colour
blue

striped cap
tied underneath her chin

striped bathing suit

from
around her neck

around her arms

down
to her knees

she swam
old-fashioned
in a kind of crawl
she swam
the sky away

until the night time
and the ocean
of black

then she turned

a minor lane change

and her guide became
the evening star

while she swam on
in a kind of
old fashioned
crawl
away again

it is

there is more
than form

there is more
than words

there is more than
just the writing

there is the line
the fine line
holding things together

linking to the heart

tangling up
around the spirit

embroiling the sound
of it

to
make the hymn

to
sing the song

to cry out loud

      L-A-A-A-A!

it is more
than the form

much more
than the words

purified

in the dream
he positioned himself
to stand
facing the breeze
that crossed his little fire

picking up
the twirl of smoke
rising from the bark
the sticks
the leaves he had offered
for the burning

>*the smell of smoke*
>*the acridness*
>*is the taste*
>*of flame*
>*that has spent all it has*
>*dancing*
>*within the yellow light*

>*the grey rising*
>*is a billow of the spirit*
>*now begun its journey*

>*high away*
>*high away*

he stood in a dream
let the smoke
pass through him

a filtering that left him clean

and tasting
of the dance of flames

>*high away*
>*high away*

the water

> *what am I to drink*
>
> *bad water*
>
> *how will I ease my thirst*
>
> *bad water*

she stared
a long time
down
into the mud

still a gleam
of moisture
reflected
by a high sun

less than a thimble
coloured grey
coloured brown
in shallow depressions
coloured sludge

soft sludge

> *what am I to drink*
>
> *what am I to do*
>
> *how will I ease my thirst*
>
> *bad water*

she recalled a day
of green grass
here

she recalled
a waterhole

she remembered this place
in colours
that were alive

she remembered . . .

too long ago
now

she remembered
the colour
pure
of clean water

>   *what am I to drink*
>
>   *bad water*
>
>   *how will I ease my thirst*
>
>   *bad water*

an ocean of purity : one drop of passion

the water was pure
distilled
through soil
and sand
and stone

taken
from a spring
that bubbled up
spontaneously
from the ground
en route
to a stream

en route
to a river

he held
above the beaker
a vial
a dropper
filled with a passion
of violet

what
is a drop

one drop

it is a small thing

hardly significant

and
in the scheme
of things
of no matter

no matter
at all

one drop

spread
like a purple cloud
billowing down from where
it bounced
back into the air
then landed again

liquid smoke
boiling toward the bottom

the beaker
was unchanged

one drop
amounts to nothing
in the body
of a beaker

and the water
that pure
clean
clear
spring water

remained transparent

was still
water yes
still obviously water
and yet changed

un-pure
and
tainted

pure water

> *sprinkle me with water*
>
> *pure water*
>
> *I will then*
> *be clean*
>
> *sprinkle me with water*
> *spring water*
>
> *I will then*
> *be clean*
>
> *sprinkle me with . . .*

it is symbolic
of course

what is water
what is
pure

how much do you need
to be washed
clean

perhaps
only a drop
on an open palm
while in the mind
in the soul
a deluge

> *sprinkle me with water*
> *rose water*
>
> *sprinkle me*
> *that I*
> *be clean*

difficult departure

he did not flinch
when the smoke
rose up

did not move
when it passed
seemingly
right through him

even though
his soul was touched
by taint
as the body burned

he did not flinch
but had the taste
of ashes
felt
the corpse-touch
the corpse-grasp

even as
the body burned

he realized
after
he could feel his heart
erratically beating

realized after
how much he'd held on
to his breath

shaky
a little dizzy
he walked
from the remnant pyre

An Ocean Of Purity

in a line
undeviating
he walked
toward the river

palpitations still
in his chest
sweat beads
on his brow
nausea
rising up
within him

he did not stop
at the edge
of the water

he did not stop
disrobed
flinging
as he walked

step by step
he descended
feeling the water rise

then slowly
methodically
he rubbed his skin

word (1) holding

wherever she went
people began to notice
one hand
always
closed tightly

fingers in a clench
hand in a fist
as though frozen

as though her arm —
her good right arm —
ended
in a club-head

and she
always distracted
preoccupied
muttering to herself

> *keep it closed*
>
> *hold it tight*
>
> *don't let it go*

like a struggle
in her mind
that was a struggle
in her hand

> *hold it in*

it got so
she could not see anymore
and it got so
she could not hear

An Ocean Of Purity

it got so
all that she could do
was sit
on the floor
against the walls
of a corner
gently rocking

one hand
holding
the fist of the other

muttering

> *don't*
> *let*
> *it go*

word (2) secret

a word of power
is a small thing
is
everything

small enough
he concealed it
in the palm
of an up-curled hand

glances

glimpses

he opened out his hand
gazed a little moment
closed into a fist
again

shhh

it is a secret
there is no sharing

shhh

to keep a secret
wants only
one

he closed her hand
into a fist
again

> *you want to*
> *take a look*
> *at power . . .*
>
> *well*
> *you can take a look*
> *at this*

nothing sweet

he drank somewhere
sometime
of corrupted water

he found
once upon his lips
that it tasted
sweet

there it is

there you go

it doesn't take
a lot
to drag you back
again

he's a drinker now
nothing does
but the taste of sweet

he no longer knows
what clean water
is

but it seems
to him
like nothing

clear
pure
nothing

one last drop (to do some good)

the universe
is complete

vast and dynamic
it stretches out
and around

it reaches
everywhere

the heart
is where she places herself
with a beaker held
in each hand

contemplating

contemplating

there is room left
creative room left
for another drop
just one

but
which . . .

the swirling
in the beaker of the left
is dark
and clouded

the liquid that she holds
on her right
is transparent

clear

there is room left
in the universe
for one drop . . .

for one drop more
and
for its consequences

she ponders

she contemplates

will, of water

the water will
flow down stream

the water will
will not flow
up

how strong is
the water

how very strong
is will
much stronger
maybe
than will not

will not
the water

down
is the chosen one
and so

and so
water will

flow

cleansed

she held her hand out
for soap

I placed on it
a bubble —
one tiny bubble —
of rainbow coloured sud

she accepted with a small bow
and then
elaborately began
to rub her hands together
as though lathering

>*her arms*

>*her body*

>*more lather*

>*her legs*
>*her face*
>*her hair*

when she was done
she dipped
into a bucket
that I swear
was dry

and rinsed herself

all the supposed lather
off

stood
and shook herself
like a wetted hound

turned back to me
and bowed again
thank you

then she walked
serene
away
completely cleansed

losing sight of pure

after months
he had his array
of shaped mirrors

he lined them up
outside
on a sunny day

he angled one
the first
to catch the sun's rays

reflected the light
up
reflected the light
down

each mirror
removed
an impurity
from the light

so the ray
bouncing the line
grew whiter

grew brighter

became unbearable
in its intensity

the end of the line
was an empty jar

a phial
of sorts

he fiddled in his pocket
with the lid
while he tracked the light
as it grew hard
white

luminous
and pure

gradually
diminishing in its mass
commensurate to the increase
in clarity
as it left particles of itself
elements
behind
then the jar
then
the stopper

nothing
but the bright light

he could not resist

held it up
before him
and gazed
fully
upon it

the light
that one
pure
light
burned

but he
was blind

stirring the soup

she sat
in a quiet meditation

ladle in her hand

cauldron
before her

for a moment

nothing

for a moment

nothing

eventually
she roused herself

brought her mind back
from away
yonder
to the here-and-now
waiting
at her feet

she wondered
briefly
which direction

clock

counter-clock

all one
all one

she inserted the ladle
gently
at the very outside
edge

gripped it with both hands
and began
to stir

a slow
steady
circular motion

to clockwise
this time

and as she turned —
laboured —
with the ladle

the soup
of stars
and of stuff
began a slow

slow

spin

effects of the fountain

he'd slept
a draggled sleep

waking
he is
partly
still in the disturbance
of his dreams

uncomfortable dreams
that linger about him
cloyingly

half aware
of the sensation
of choking
on his own breath
in some moment
caught between snort
and snore

half aware
that he is in daylight
now

it is a stagger
that leads him
stumbling and half blind
around the house
wearing
still
his crumpled nightshirt

to kitchen
to ease a dry mouth
sticky

to toilet
to relieve
while still dreaming

to bathroom

the sound of water
pitched hard
from showerhead
to floor

the taste of steam
rising

he strips off
the nightshirt
and steps forward
into the pelting sting

and begins to feel

alive

in this world

he puts his head
under the downpour
and is subsumed

hears
feels
only water surrounding him

feels the wash
of life

clean life

new

all over him

he begins to sing

water

I see through you
as though
you are not there

hold you
in the palm of my hand

you run
away

leave me
feeling
as the wind
kisses me dry

eat you
swish you
wash you down

cold
I make you warmer
until you could be
a part
of what I am

I cannot tell
you
from me

no longer you

no me

fall over me
strike me down
splash
fall away
but
don't leave me
I need you so

you
can see through me

in the palm
of my hands
you
hold me

failure oceanic

ocean
you have failed me

because water
you are not

water
is a clean thing
a soft

a pure

you
are brack

I drink you
poison

ocean you do not
serve me
you are not my friend
water

water
who sustains me
water
who is so
sweet

ocean
you are salt
and brine

you are
distasteful

ocean
what are you there for

why
are you here at all

why exist

you
with your silvered fish
so slippery

you
who are no spring
and no river

what are you
ocean

you
have failed me

only clean

to be white

the state of grace

white
is white
un-tainted

~

to make clean

to reclaim
by dint of effort

as white
as white
un-soft

~

the difference
is innocence

the difference
is lost

white is white
but clean
is only
clean

from storyland

I
will
sit
at your feet
and listen

every wave you wash
up
onto the shore
will tell me

all of your
stories
come from far away
from
distant places

foreign tongues
and
foreign fruits

your flotsam
illustrations

this timber

    ssshhaaa ssshhh

a coconut

    ssshhaaa ssshhh

a life preserver
red and white
and named for some lost
vessel

a sailing craft

> *ssshhaaa ssshhh*

> *ssshhaaa ssshhh*

I will listen
to your

> *ssshhaaa ssshhh*

quiet voice
whispering
of warmer climes

> *ssshhaaa ssshhh*

and other days

> *ssshhaaa ssshhh*

until
the moon is high

> *ssshhaaa ssshhh*

and I fall
sleeping
on my side

> *ssshhaaa ssshhh*

a hillock
one small hillock
of grains left
by the tide

> *ssshhaaa ssshhh*

> *ssshhaaa ssshhh*

a pillow come
from story land

washed all the way from
your
story land

    ssshhaaa ssshhh

I
will
sleep

your stories

    ssshhh

your stories
in my dreams

an uncoordination of gods

the god of light
spent half his time
turned
to face away

the goddess of darkness
danced then
swirling
her broad veil —
the rhapsody of night —
until he turned back
and smiled

    a dazzle

    overwhelming

the god of trees
spoke

    that's the way

    and some warm now
    please

the goddess of time
said

    either way

    half is half
    fair
    is fair

the god of storms
cried aloud

    THUNDER!

and strobed
while cloistered
inside a cloud

he was brooding

boiling

irritable
in his demeanor

and no one else could
stand those moods
but the rain

always falling

rising

    one day

she thought

    one day

    the god
    of everything . . .

she had no more
thought
than that

a thought
that was the mist
of a rising vapour

measuring

how strong are you?

*how hard
will you fight?*

*what is it
you are made of?*

*I wish to measure you
as a man*

I am strong
enough
to carry the weight
of my burden

I will fight
hard enough
to survive
through a dark night
and still rise up
to every morning

I am made
of stuff

salt water in my flesh

I am made
of moral fibre

and I will battle you
if I must
until I die

that
is the measure of me

I
am a man

the resistance

all the reeds are bowed
yielding
moving to the strength
of the wind

    yield
    yield
    yield

and then return

one reed
against the wind
bending
pushing into the strength
of the wind

    stand
    stand
    stand

be
the resistance

rehearsing the wind

she planted her feet
slightly apart
achieving
an easy balance

her posture was bent
leaning forwards
determined and strong

steadfast

she moved
half lift half shuffle
a heavy-booted foot
and with a kind of staggered roll
she clumped forward

one step

at the same time
maneuvering her stocks
to ensure
she retained balance

her clothing
overall
was cumbersome
bulky
but
in the prevailing conditions
she thought it necessary
to be well prepared

she took a quick
second step
almost
over balancing
but . . .

no

she was getting the hang
of this

in control
of her movements

another step

the stocks

another step

before long
she had successfully traversed
the length
of her lounge room

almost now
she felt ready
to go outside
and defeat the wind

ambivalent water

he did not know
to rise
or fall

ambivalent water

ambivalent man

not stone
not fish
not floating bird

his every down
led up

his every up
attempted down

in truth
the water
was not ambivalent

in truth
the water
did not care

the water is
and he
upon it

within it

resolution comes
in time
within the slap
of a wave

born of tides

she *became*
in a cottage
close by the sea

at the height
of a king tide

in the glorious heart
of a storm

she grew there

of the sand
and of the water

attuned to the moods
and movements

she became aware
early
of the power

limited
but strong

no more than twice
on any day
but
always twice
on any day

she could be seen
standing still
in concentration
for long minutes

eyes closed

hands outstretched
towards the water

and then . . .

spent
exhausted
with nothing to show

but the fishermen
watched

they knew

she was their rod
and surety

she had always known
and twice
in a day
she would stand
facing the water

the ocean bled

it was the sea
that ran
through her veins

when she opened himself —
by cut —
to bleed
she bled the ocean

she bled the brine
that flowed to fill
the lowly places

she bled
until the waters
returned

a tide to lap her feet

two challenges (1) the child at war

he commanded the waves
like an emperor

    go back

    go back

and the sea
obedient
ceased its ascent

retreated

he pursued
like wrath

an avenging angel
in pursuit
and shouting

    back

    you
    go back

and when the sea
was low
he halted

the sea halted

he turned
during the pause
and ran back
to his position
laughing

while the sea re-gathered
for the next
assault

two challenges (2) the turbulent green

she stood out
on the furthest outcropping
of rock
known by the locals as

   the slippery fish

here
the water crashed
spilling white spume
high
above the green
and white
of turbulent water

so high
that each new wave
slapped around her

saluted
eye-to-eye

before retreating

from time to time
a wave
a big wave
would wash higher

tugging at her feet

dragging

before subsiding
for a smaller set
of slaps and sprays

but ever hungry

An Ocean Of Purity

she stood
for an age
on the rocky edge

staring intently
into the green

turned abruptly
as one last wave
washed up at her
and walked away

the champion

young man

he sizes up
his journey

forward
back

forward
back

he rocks
until
he is balanced

ready

now
he starts his run

he starts
to run

he runs

the path ends
at a board

a pit
of sand

he leaps

metres

metres

into the air
he flies

lands

feet first

a forward roll

the long jump
long leap
long flight

the victor

~

the young man
standing
on the bank
of a small creek

not big
not wide
but running

gurgling

rushing water
ready to sweep away
the careless

he steps back

retreats
another step

unsure
the width
the depth
the speed
the risk
the rush

and then
he runs

one step
two

and another

he runs

he leaps

he lands
on the other side

the victor

the champion

it was only
a creek

not so very large

but . . .

he leapt it

he is
the champion

Bachelard Source Materials

Gaston Bachelard, French Philosopher lived from 27 June 1884 to 16 October 1962. The series of poems and poetry in this book has drawn inspiration from the following publications by Bachelard, translated into English.

Intuition of the Instant by Gaston Bachelard (1932) Eileen Rizo-Patron (Translator) Northwestern University Press, 2013

The New Scientific Spirit, by Gaston Bachelard (1934), A. Goldhammer (Translator) Beacon Pr; 1st Edition (1984)

The Psychoanalysis of Fire, by Gaston Bachelard (1938), A.C. Ross (Translator) (1964).

Lautréamont, Gaston Bachelard (1939), Robert S. Dupree (Author), James Hillman (Author), Dallas Institute Publications; Reprint Edition (2012)

Water and Dreams: An Essay on the Imagination of Matter by Gaston Bachelard (1942), Edith R. Farrell (Translator) (1983.

Air and Dreams: An Essay on the Imagination of Movement, by Gaston Bachelard (1943), Edith R. Farrell (Translator), Frederick Farrell (Translator) Dallas Institute Publication Dallas Institute Publications (1988)

Earth and Reveries of Will: An Essay on the Imagination of Matter by Gaston Bachelard (1943), Kenneth Haltman (Translator) Dallas Institute Publications (2002)

Earth and Reveries of Repose: An Essay on Images of Interiority by Gaston Bachelard (1948), Mary McAllester Jones (Translation), Dallas Institute Publications (2011)

Dialectic of Duration. Gaston Bachelard (1950), Mary McAllester Jones (Translator), Rowman & Littlefield Publishers; (2016)

The Poetics of Space by Gaston Bachelard (1958), Maria Jolas (Translator) Penguin Classics (1964).

The Poetics of Reverie, by Gaston Bachelard (1960), Daniel Russell (Translator) Beacon Press; New Ed Edition (1971)

The Flame of a Candle, by Gaston Bachelard, (1961), Joni Caldwell (Translator) Dallas Institute Publications (1988).

The Right to Dream by Gaston Bachelard (1970), J.A. Underwood

(Translator) Dallas Institute Publications (1988)
Fragments of a Poetics of Fire, by Gaston Bachelard, Kenneth Haltman (Translator), Dallas Institute Publications (1988)
On Poetic Imagination and Reverie, by Gaston Bachelard, Colette Gaudin (Translator) Spring Publications; (2014)

Author Information

Frank Prem has been a storytelling poet for more than forty years and spent his working life in various parts of the public psychiatry system in Victoria, Australia.

His work has been published in magazines, e-zines, and anthologies both in Australia and internationally, and he has performed and recorded his poetry as spoken word. He has published more than 35 poetry and picture-book collections.

Frank is an Adjunct Research Associate with the School of Education at Charles Sturt University, Australia. He and his wife live in the beautiful township of Beechworth, in north-east Victoria.

Connect with Frank

Find Frank at his website www.FrankPrem.com, or through Social Media online at Facebook, X (Twitter), Instagram and YouTube.

Other Published Works

Free Verse Poetry

Small Town Kid (2018)
Devil In The Wind (2019)
The New Asylum (2019)
Herja, Devastation - With Cage Dunn (2019)
Walk Away Silver Heart (2020)
A Kiss for the Worthy (2020)
Rescue and Redemption (2020)
Pebbles to Poems (2020)
The Garden Black (2022)
A Specialist at The Recycled Heart (2022)
Ida: Searching for The Jazz Baby (2023)
From Volyn to Kherson (2023)
Alive Is What You Feel (2023)
White Whale (2024)
Pilgrim Volume 1 - Illustrated by Leanne Murphy (2024)
A Poetry Archive Volume 1 (2024)
A Poetry Archive Volume 2 (2024)
A Poetry Archive Volume 3 (2024)
A Poetry Archive Volume 4 (2024)

Picture Poetry/Spoken Image

Voices (In The Trash) (2020)
The Beechworth Bakery Bears (2021)
Sheep On The Somme (2021)
Waiting For Frank-Bear (2021)
A Lake Sambell Walk (2021)
A Few Places Near Home (2023)
The Cielonaut (2024)

What Readers Say

Small Town Kid

A modern-day minstrel. Highly recommended.
  —A. F. (Australia)

Small Town Kid is a wonderful collection.
  —S. T. (Australia)

Devil In The Wind

Trust me, this book will stay with you. Bravo!
  —K. K. (USA)

Moving, beautiful, and terrible. I was left with a profound sense of respect, as well as a reminder that we should never take for granted every precious every moment of life.
  —J. S. (South Africa)

The New Asylum

Words can't do justice to the emotional journey I travelled in (reading this collection).
  —C. D. (Australia)

If I had to pick one book over the past year that has truly resonated with me, this would be it.
  —K. B. (USA)

Walk Away Silver Heart

Instantly grips you by the throat in his step-by-step story of survival. Bravo!
  —K. K. (USA)

Outstanding!
  —B. T. (Australia)

A Kiss For The Worthy

A Celebration of Life Written in Thoughtful Bursts of Poetic Expression
—C M C (United States)

With every verse, I found myself reflecting about myself, my life, and the world.
—K

Rescue and Redemption

The passion of love in its many forms explored by one for another.
—J L (United States)

I've enjoyed every word, every breath. Every moment within the life of these stories.
—C D (Australia)

Sheep On The Somme

Museums and archivists take note~sell this in your gift shops, preserve it in your archives. Professors, teachers~share with your students.
—A R C (United States)

(This) book is a beautiful and graphic tribute to all those brave men and women who gave their lives for their countries between 1914 and 1918.
—R C (South Africa)

Ida: Searching for The Jazz Baby

I found myself deeply moved by the presentation of Ida's elusive, illusionary life.
—E G (United States)

He gives her a depth and vulnerability that the press didn't.
— A C (United Kingdom

The Garden Black

Prem creates verse that illuminates our world, its experiences and history.

—S C (United Kingdom)

Prem's poetry reminds that life is fragile and fleeting ... both harsh and beautiful.

—D G K (Canada)

A Few Places Near Home

The author has captured many beautiful images in this book, and is a wonderful photographer as well as a poet. This book would make a beautiful coffee table book filled with moving prose to make us ponder with gorgeous accompanying images.

—D K (Canada)

www.FrankPrem.com

www.ingramcontent.com/pod-product-compliance
Lightning Source LLC
Chambersburg PA
CBHW052213090526
44584CB00020BA/3167